Growth Hackers

*Maximizing Company Expansion in the
Digital Era*

Joseph H. Carillo

Disclaimer

This book has been written for information purposes only. Every effort has been made to make this ebook as complete and accurate as possible. However, there may be mistakes in typography or content. Also, this book provides information only up to the publishing date. Therefore, this ebook should be used as a guide - not as the ultimate source.

The purpose of this ebook is to educate. The author and the publisher does not warrant that the information contained in this e-book is fully complete and shall not be responsible for any errors or omissions. The author and publisher shall have neither liability nor responsibility to any person or entity with respect to any loss or damage caused or alleged to be caused directly or indirectly by this book.

Table of Contents

Introduction

Growth hacking started as a trend but is now essential. Expansion hacking is vitally essential for providing goods and services to clients in light of the Internet's ever-expanding expansion.

Years ago, while programmers were entirely in control of inputting and creating code, or a platform, marketers were in charge of pushing items. But now, these phrases have combined to form a singular method of genuine development called "growth hacking."

Although marketing will always be necessary, it's crucial to have one person or a small group of staff concerned with the business's specific expansion.

The Internet has given companies a brand-new means to expand, often apparently overnight. Because product attributes may contribute directly to growth, consumers no longer have to feel deceived by-products.

Growth hackers are aware of these factors and that sales are good news and distribution routes are no longer A to B.

As a result of the channels that social media has produced, channels are currently being shifted or even established. This may include brand-new websites or well-read blogs written by prominent people outside the entertainment industry. Growth hacking will eventually be adopted into even the biggest enterprises, although it is now thought to revolve around startups.

In this manual, I'll go into great depth on how you may use the power of the Internet to expand your company, create your portfolio, and establish your brand.

Chapter 1

Basics of Internet Marketing

In essence, Internet marketing gets people to go to a given website, download a specific app, or buy a specific item.

Most people working in the Internet marketing industry often have backgrounds in either business or the IT sector, depending on whether a company or individual chooses to recruit a specific person or small group of people.

However, as technology has advanced, marketers and programmers have combined to create growth hackers who can develop firms more quickly than before.

Working long hours in stifling classrooms or the rear of congested offices is no longer necessary for Internet marketing. Instead, being a frequent Internet user will teach you the fundamentals. If people detest using computers, no education will be useful.

People that love using emerging social media

platforms, have a business mindset, enjoy buying and selling things online, and enjoy blogging are excellent examples of people who have the potential to become great growth hackers. These real-world experience examples enable newbies to stand out from the competition rapidly.

Creating a portfolio is one of the first things to consider when entering the growth hacking field. Creating a portfolio entails.

There are many factors to consider, but the fundamental concept is to highlight your finest and most relevant work.

This is crucial when putting together a portfolio to send to other professionals or applying for a specific job. To sell yourself effectively, you should develop a marketing portfolio that highlights your prior accomplishments and your potential for future greatness in a particular industry.

Internet marketers who want to become growth hackers need to discover a specialized specialty to concentrate on in addition to building a credible portfolio. There are several approaches and tactics to consider when looking for a niche to enter. Most experts advise concentrating on a niche in which the parties involved already demonstrate interest.

The advantages of long-tail keywords, which concentrate on several little units rather than one huge or extremely popular unit or product, should be used in conjunction with studying the ins and outs of a given topic.

There are four proven ways to succeed when starting the earliest stages of growth hacking after an awareness of a reliable portfolio's fundamental components and identifying a particular niche to focus on research.

Firms must first build connections with their prospective clients to achieve long-term success with any of these four strategies. The other strategies include content marketing and direct response copywriting, essential for understanding growth marketing.

The last and maybe most crucial stage is to create a worthwhile offering that people will want to share. Using the Growth hacking becomes more feasible if the four success principles are understood, and the following actions need a more direct commitment.

True growth hackers know that virality is not a result of chance but rather an intentional reaction to tactical and analytical development. By requesting favors that don't appear like favors, growth hackers may genuinely persuade customers to tell others about their company or product. Our partnership will focus on strategies used by massive daily deal companies Groupon and LivingSocial.

It's crucial to remember that growth hackers only concentrate on objectives that can be achieved. The best analytics are then used to thoroughly examine these objectives, leveraging strengths and evaluating shortcomings to provide the best outcomes.

Development hackers start with a hypothesis and continually evaluate and re-try experiments to uncover the best solutions for ever-expanding company development, much like the scientific process.

One has to fully comprehend the consumer's psyche to genuinely hack development. Think of website visitors as a filter or funnel. Growth hackers entice a variety of visitors to a website, when they arrive, they screen them to determine which ones are able and ready to make a purchase, subscribe to a mailing list, or access other lucrative content.

Growth hackers ensure that no opportunity for profit or growth is missed from the beginning to the end.

The filter may then be dismantled after a thorough analysis. All visitors are welcomed to be drawn in by several degrees of enticement at the funnel's extended open mouth, which serves as its entrance.

These pull strategy types include Free resources and awards, enticing people to enter their own free choice. Gaining visitors is not a coincidence, and growth hackers know the best ways to attract, motivate, and close sales.

There are push strategies in addition to pull approaches, and they will be covered in more depth throughout the book. In contrast to passively waiting for a visitor to drop by, these push strategies go for the customer.

These strategies are best summed up as an advertisement appearing before a video on a popular website. Although all of these approaches are useful, none is as useful as the options offered by the production technique.

Product tactics are growth strategies where customers utilize the interface to spread the word about a product or service. All social networking platforms, including Facebook, Gmail, LinkedIn, and Twitter, would fall under this category.

Essentially, these goods sell themselves because you and your friends must be on the same service or plan to interact and live in that social plane.

Chapter 2

Creating a Portfolio

The optimum time to start a portfolio is always right away, regardless of the question. It's never too early to start, and there is only upward movement for people who are completely new to a profession.

The fundamental concept is to start a portfolio with plans to regularly update and improve the work to constantly show off an individual's finest performance, whether people are looking for one for writing, graphic design, or internet marketing.

Marketing portfolios often rely on the kind of future employment that the applicant hopes to get. While it may seem insignificant to start a portfolio, for some people, marketing will get started with a personally managed website. It's important to remember that while others are browsing the managed site, outsiders may seek advice, and it's always best to be ready for an opportunity.

When updating your portfolio, job seekers should consider the sort of internship or position they want to apply for. In general, it's ideal to compile the finest work in a style that will impress most employers, honest, true, and straightforward in the most practical way feasible.

Making the Most of Your Chances

Writing is crucial in any industry, including Internet marketing. Others who thrive in writing distinguish themselves from others who seem trapped in a specific level or sector.

Correct language and tone are often indicators of both patience and knowledge. An incorrect term or phrase in a portfolio's conversation is similar to spelling a word incorrectly on a job application or resume.

It's crucial to show strategic thought in addition to good writing. Even if it seems challenging to include in a portfolio, consider how you might stand out from the competition.

Analyze the scenario, whether it is a campaign, a partnership, or a novel company approach. In addition to coming up with anything fresh, it's crucial to comprehend the state of the world right now to fully grasp Internet marketing.

Lastly, be careful to accurately portray the portfolio's volume and quality of work. Make sure to showcase the amount of effort in your finest goods by showcasing the greatest work, whether you have recently graduated from college and just have work from school or have been working as a freelancer for a month or ten years.

After showcasing your greatest qualities, you may identify what you want to accomplish in the future of marketing and advertising.

Future Definition

The major goal of a marketing portfolio is to show the measures being made to define a future profession, even if it is straightforward to emphasize the previous. Anything in a portfolio that isn't exceptional will show a lack of devotion to potential employers.

Consider revising prior work to your current degree of excellence utilizing any tips and techniques you have learned as you advance and thrive as a professional.

Consider even producing work you want to provide

in the future rather than relying on your present output. For instance, a writer whose profession is mostly nonfiction may write fiction in his or her spare time and include both genres in the portfolio.

The portfolio's variety will be better shown, and the person's versatility as a freelancer will be highlighted, even if there may not be the same demand to perform as there is to deliver to an editor.

Freelance Work And Internships

Even those who didn't go to college or who changed fields after graduation might benefit from beginning with internships and freelancing while attempting to join the world of paid labor.

With only a few examples, one may start a freelancing job. Alternatively, one could apply for an internship and work professionally in a busy setting.

Working at an internship might help you promote yourself as someone who keeps your word and meets deadlines. Any completed work can assist in developing a portfolio, whether you are working alone or in a group on a project.

If you ever find yourself working in a collaborative context, be careful to mention formally the precise parts of the project to which you directly contributed.

After developing your portfolio, you'll discover you're more certain in meetings. Imagine yourself in a circumstance where you will be questioned, and you will be able to immediately reference a sample from your portfolio. Being prepared with this information can help you obtain employment and establish credibility within the first few minutes of any contact.

Never forget to create your finest portfolio and maintain it currently to get unexpected opportunities and advance your career as a skilled Internet marketer.

Chapter 3

Choosing a Niche

The latest and greatest infomercials advertising the newest must-have gadget of the season will usually result in people rolling their eyes and exhaling heavily.

Predicting the gadget of the season may be tough because it can be challenging to envisage the perfect product for the general public and because it is sometimes practically impossible to create the perfect device. Consider meeting demand by spending the time to do research and fill a specialized sector rather than attempting to manufacture demand.

Nothing is more distressing than developing a new product only to learn that it has already been created but was so badly promoted that no one has ever heard of it.

While many amazing goods have been developed in this manner in the past, the foundation we now have in place for popularizing new items makes it challenging to be the greatest in any particular industry owing to a variety of fierce competitors. Instead, think about identifying an existing market and developing a product that that group of people will only purchase.

Think about finding a specialty that fascinates your work. For instance, while having an innovative concept for a new baby sling, a male collegiate athlete is unlikely to be able to advise others in his demographic on the finest fitness gear or what stay-at-home mothers require for their daily routines.

The biggest benefit of remaining in your demographic is that you will be familiar with the questions to ask and the issues to initially avoid. At least when establishing a firm or developing a new product, consider adhering to the customs of your target market.

Think About the Extremes

Consider some of the most detailed and precise companies you've seen online or in a favorite magazine. A marathon runner started Photo Finish Frames as a framing company, but it swiftly transitioned to producing specialty frames for runners.

In essence, the owner created a mechanism to send a precise size frame to a marathon runner so that the runner's picture, race number, and finishing time could be framed.

Another example of a specialty is No Film School. This kind of website sends concise, weekly emails. The emails from No Film School appear as a week's worth of twenty pieces.

Every one of these articles is written with prospective filmmakers who are curious about the inner workings of screenplay, camera, lighting, production, and all the other areas that result in independent filmmaking outside of Hollywood in mind.

Simply put, this market encourages regular film education without incurring crippling student loan debt.

Choosing a Niche

Because not everyone is interested in marathon running or independent filmmaking, these two businesses have succeeded in their respective industries.

Consider looking at the social circles you currently belong to build a new business that you would be eager to be a part of, either as an owner or a member, rather than continuing to dream of starting a company that already exists.

Take a creative look at your present résumé, social media profile, interests, professional experience, and daily exercise routine. If you want more inspiration, try joining new organizations that interest you and examine all the groups you have ever been a member of.

This might entail genuine clubs, magazine subscriptions, or frequently visited websites. Then, consider others like yourself and examine what you appreciate, why you enjoy it, and those who may value similar things.

Narrowing Your Search

After thoroughly listing all the areas you are interested in, choose the two that intrigue you the most. A product may sometimes fall under more than one category, but starting with two is ideal for generating a greater variety of ideas.

Once you've decided on two categories, do further study. To find more information about a certain area of interest, browse websites that concentrate on particular categories or go to a nearby bookshop.

While picking a category for the affluent, like golf, is not crucial, picking one for those who buy products related to a field—like runners or photographers who buy shoes and equipment—is crucial.

Once you've decided on two distinct markets, start developing concepts for items that don't yet exist or have been badly promoted.

Consider identifying current issues and easy fixes for them using a simple product. Consider how groundbreaking and crucial the windshield wiper was to the first automobile.

Be Specific

Consider the advantage to be obtained or the issue that the product is attempting to solve, sometimes even before the product's first version is built. The product has to be succinctly stated in a single phrase, much like choosing the right tagline for a movie, to eliminate any chance of the advantage of the product not being understood by prospective buyers.

Take the original Apple iPod release as an example. The firm simply supplied "1,000 songs in your pocket" rather than mentioning gigabytes or other technical terminology that many customers find confusing.

Long-Tail Keyword Search

The long tail of keywords might then be the emphasis of a sales site after developing a profitable product or service. The word comes from statistics, but the idea is still quite straightforward.

When offering many individual online searches or considering sales of a huge number of distinctive products, the phrase refers to the retail.

In other words, it might be challenging for a new business to appear in the top results on a Google page, but it's simpler to rank higher when searches are more focused.

Take real estate as an example to better comprehend

the long tail. There is intense competition for the top results when using SEO keywords like "real estate."

Results are significantly more focused when you use terms like "Winston Salem North Carolina Real Estate townhouse," however. These firms concentrate on the details rather than employing broad, generic words.

By concentrating on hard-to-find things for specialized clients, the long tail enables firms to avoid the obligation of meeting the demand for popular items among the general public.

Companies may compete with more well-known businesses that offer a lot of popular things in bulk by increasing the overall sales of their many unique products. Among the most well-known long tail sellers, look at the bulk book sales from Amazon or the bulk movie rentals, music downloads, or book downloads from Apple.

Chapter 4

Techniques for Success

As indicated, learning Internet marketing is not simple, but it can be done. People's perception that Internet marketing is simply another "get rich quick" business strategy is a big part of its issue.

Like an athlete from a small town being picked in the first round or winning an Olympic event, there are "overnight companies," but it's easy to overlook the work required before sudden success. The fact that the public was not there for the conflict does not imply that it did not occur.

However, with the help of Internet marketing and growth hacking, companies may expand more quickly and profitably than ever before for those prepared to put in the effort.

This chapter introduces readers to a systematic approach to efficient Internet marketing. These four strategies may be the cornerstone of Internet marketing and the basis for success.

Four strategies for Internet marketing should never

be ignored, although there are many instances of advice (both good and bad).

These four core strategies—relationships, direct response copywriting, content marketing, and value products—form the basis of Internet marketing.

Relationships

Perhaps the most basic strategy is to build enduring, intimate connections with clients. It often relies on the firm in question whether this refers to a relationship between an individual and their audience.

Regardless, the approach serves as a helpful reminder to company owners that maintaining a working connection is considerably simpler than forging a new one.

Finding new clients costs money and takes time. Whether they operate a brick-and-mortar shop or an online magazine, businesses have struggled to get fresh leads for years.

Asking a regular client to return is simpler than bringing in a stranger off the street. Know the worth of your clients, and let them know it.

Providing an atmosphere worthy of their attention is crucial for this to happen. Nobody wants to return to a website that is badly run or poorly designed more than once, much like a shop with inadequate lighting.

Beyond these obvious points, keep in mind that readers and consumers alike want to see fresh content since that keeps them coming back for more, regardless of whether you're selling things or looking for readers.

By doing these actions, you'll not only have your customers returning, but you'll also get them to tell their friends about you, cutting the cost of advertising and only getting new members via word-of-mouth.

When patrons trust a brand or information source and feel appreciated, they will spread the word about it. Always respect your audience and tell them you also value them.

Respect comes from your market and your audience. Because, in essence, nothing else counts without your devoted clients, concentrate only on the audience's and the market's wants.

Put their needs ahead of the requirements of the

business, and the business will succeed based on this. Maintain a standard of quality and spread it to your clientele.

Writing Direct Response Ads

Most readers will immediately notice that the most popular websites follow social media trends and prominently display such articles, reports, and videos so visitors can locate them easily.

Since the average American's attention span has shrunk to milliseconds, highlighting the most recent content up front for potential viewers is crucial, much like showcasing fresh items in the front display of a local shop.

It is vitally essential to have effective copywriting approaches to spread the message, regardless of whether a site broadcasts current happenings or produces its own. Try to think of a catchy title that flatters and educates the reader to grab their attention.

To ensure the information sinks in, it's crucial to avoid being excessively subtle in this aspect. Many websites may even use puns to emphasize the content and make the reader grin.

After creating the ideal headline, focus on a well-written, educational, and well-placed layout. This will prompt the reader to take some kind of action, whether it be clicking on the next link on the page or continuing to the next stage of making a purchase.

These time-tested methods, formerly used by companies or newspapers decades ago, are now as effective as ever. Maintain the fundamentals of honesty and up-to-date information while using beautiful design.

Content Promotion

The next item to be delivered is excellent content after the headlines and layout. The greatest information should be delivered, together with material that is accurate linguistically and produced by reliable authors. Many freelancing websites provide outsourcing for those who are too busy to produce their content.

Once the first piece of material has been shared, it's critical to maintain doing so. There is never enough content in a few pieces here and there. Create a routine and keep delivering on time, much as you would when you would feed a pet. Stay focused and adhere to a planned content schedule to delight readers and educate newcomers.

Consider providing the reader with the advantages of a different systematized timetable and the planned information. For instance, this can provide occasional free ebooks or seasonal discounts.

Offer additional perks that arise directly in exchanging money for a product or service, discounts, and free information.

If your company fits this model, you should better advertise it by making a gift.

Important Products

Possessing a worthwhile product is the last element of the puzzle. Although it is disheartening to see someone reselling inferior items to earn a significant profit, you have no justification for doing the same. Find something worthwhile to acquire and sell for a profit if you cannot produce anything worth selling.

Even if the concept is fresh and hazy, readers probably know what they want to sell. In actuality, selling is everyone's line of work.

Individuals may make money while offering customers a valued service, whether selling ideas, services, downloads, or items.

Verify if it is worth the price indicated after discovering something genuinely worthwhile. It's critical to consider the precious worth of the reader's attention when determining the cost of a product or service.

Because public attention is such a precious resource, it must always be valued for what it is to the owner and never disregarded.

If a business requests time and attention instead of money, this time and attention must be valued equally to monetary revenue. Although it may seem less useful initially, it is the first step towards creating something worthy of notice and worth real money.

While this may sound perplexing, consider businesses like Instagram or Snapchat, to whom billions of dollars have been given for a service that has never really generated revenue as a service.

Chapter 5

Development Hacker Marketing

True growth hackers know common fallacies about online marketing and the definition of a "viral" phenomenon. Going viral seems like a chance, coincidence, or total accident to outsiders who witness an "overnight success," like all other such events.

Although viral marketing has a lot of appeal, it is not as simple as just uploading a video online. Everyone wants to become viral, but it takes more than just desire to generate significant sharing.

The first challenge for growth hackers is determining if a product or service is worth recommending or talking about. Customers are more likely to spread the word if the product is noteworthy than is typical.

If the product is worthwhile, it should also be simple to disseminate. Sharing might be accomplished via add-ons like social networking platforms in its most basic form.

Companies or people think their product is worth becoming viral when it doesn't have the hardest time getting the word out about it. It doesn't just happen that anything becomes viral. Certain items gain popularity more quickly than others because they deserve consideration and are often superior to the competition.

The Detection Of Growth Hacking

Start by considering the people sharing information about a new product. Potential customers or trend-setters need to identify a worthwhile product for their time on social media to mention or share for virality to operate.

Whether it's a straightforward copy and paste, an addition of a link, the embedding of a video, or the mention of a product, this detracts from the social experience of any one person.

This can only include asking a buddy to upload a video, share it on Facebook or Twitter, or add them as a contact for smaller companies. While talking to genuine internet pals is a great place to start, you must also be careful.

No one wants to provide a hand if a buddy comes

out as overbearing or uncaring. Instead of making it appear like a favor, ask a buddy for this huge favor. In addition to being deserving of trending, this also needs to encourage trending when it broadens your audience.

When promoting a new product, growth hacking outperforms conventional marketing. Only a few items may ever become viral, and for a product to have value, it must be desired by everyone who could use it or come into touch with it.

This only occurs when a customer trusts a product or when a product is exceptional. The term "remarkable" has lost part of its meaning in translation, but it still refers to anything noteworthy.

Turning To Become A Growth Hacker

It's crucial to remember that a growth hacker has no power to alter or enhance the product after picking one to promote. A growth hacker can do everything they can to modify a product's description but cannot alter the actual product, much like a spin doctor helping a politician. Growth hackers strive to create virality rather than residing in built-on marketing.

LivingSocial and Groupon are perhaps the top two recent instances of growth hacking. These two daily deal websites provide a superb marketing strategy, a never-ending supply of items, and exclusive discounts.

LivingSocial provides a "Get this deal for free" option that asks users to refer three friends to any bargain through a unique link in exchange for a free item for the original user, regardless of the deal's price. When a buddy uses the "Refer a friend" feature on Groupon and makes a purchase, Groupon will credit the user with $10.

These instances range greatly from something as straightforward as "Like this on Facebook" buttons, which certainly provide users the opportunity to promote the goods but provide no meaningful motivation.

By joining up only three friends, the LivingSocial example shows how a user may get a free vacation. Compared to merely liking something on Facebook, these daily deal websites save much money on advertising and provide far more gratifying leads. Instead of gambling with squandered advertising dollars, these two deals involve paying users.

The excellent (but failing) business Dropbox launched a "Get free space" option soon after these two websites were live to get more customers to adopt their cloud-based storage solution.

Any further friends who signed up for the program would get 500 megabytes for every new buddy that joined. Following many months of difficulty, Dropbox saw a roughly 60% surge in sign-ups, with around 2.8 million direct invitations repeating every month. Currently, recommendations still account for 35% of all sales.

The Use Of Email Services

The straightforward Hotmail notion of adding a line at the bottom of an email is now used by Gmail and Mailbox. Hotmail would, in this case, write "PS: I love you—Get Free Email," which greatly aided the company's growth—it reached around a million users in the first six months after going live.

The firm quickly increased and sold to Microsoft

35

for around $400 million. Similar thinking was put out by Google but with the addition of an invite-only situation.

These crucial measures outweigh using a PR agency since they start inside the company and spread outside. These companies develop from the inside in such a way that they control both the product's outside appearance and its internal operations.

In essence, these organizations are giving out free information or goods to just assist the business in spreading the word about the goods and services that consumers already value.

Not just any item or film can instantly be sent to millions. For the community to share anything, there must be a compelling cause. Virulence is a planned process, not an accident.

Chapter 6

Process for Hacking Steps

Like any successful business, starting with a focused focus on precise, attainable objectives is preferable. Focusing on a large enough range renders it meaningless due to its nebulousness. Additionally, although obtaining enormous growth is undoubtedly the desired outcome, completing smaller tasks must first build it.

Like driving a vehicle on a lengthy trip, the destination is only reached after fully comprehending the road.

Once prospective growth hackers have established a reasonable, achievable objective, the following stage is to deploy analytics to monitor the progress of goals.

In the absence of exact analytics, objectives are fundamentally meaningless.

Of course, it is possible to accomplish certain objectives without an outline, but the organization is essential for success. Analytics provide a conclusive response to demonstrate whether a goal has been attained.

They also provide the details needed to indicate which elements should be altered to test a different hypothesis. Like a sculptor, the unneeded components must be removed to achieve the ultimate outcome.

After analytics have been implemented, the next stage is to assess the startup or business to see which components may be used as leverage for the enterprise.

Every corporation has the potential to have something distinctive that will assist in defining or improving the organization. Using mass email marketing as an example usually, the question contains the solution. Some businesses might need one approach, while others need a different one.

Always prioritize developing your strengths while planning for expansion, and remember that every firm has a unique fulcrum for its unique leverage.

Making a hypothesis is the best course of action before continuing. A hypothesis is a calculated estimate of prospective outcomes from a technique much to the scientific method.

Start the experiment after outlining the hypothesis. Avoid being naive while performing any experiment when considering the resources needed for the expected results.

Do not expect the organization to have fewer users if it needs thousands. Learn from any achievements or mistakes once all the data has been collected and the resources have been coordinated, and keep in mind that the data will only supply information if you are willing to utilize it.

In both science and business, experiments are intended to be carried out repeatedly until they are successful. This could just need minor adjustments or extensive renovation.

When utilizing email marketing, think about setting up a control group. This group will assist in monitoring the external environmental parameters that are more challenging to monitor in even the best conditions.

It's critical to understand when an external element significantly impacts a product's sales. Think about businesses that want to grow in a different part of the globe but discover that their goods offend specific cultural features. Without a control group to help focus the findings, they can be disregarded and considered a failure.

Finally, be sure to carry out the procedure again. While some tests are unsuccessful, others just need minor adjustments. Utilize the data and carry out further tests till you are successful.

The solution is often within reach, so keep looking for a successful growth hack if you believe in your product and your business, much like the gold hunter giving up his dig inches from riches.

Growth Hacking Myths

Ignore the technical language and consider what it means to be a growth hacker in its purest form if the steps above seem unfamiliar. Since the term first surfaced in 2010, it has been misused and overused by too many individuals.

Similar to a new fad term, this phrase is soon linked to other expressions and incorrect views. Browse the following to discover the misconceptions behind the buzz rather than continuing to think it's exclusively for certain sorts of individuals.

It's crucial to first realize that a growth hacker need not be a coder or a conventional marketer. Marketers must significantly define and restrict their sector to become a growth hacker.

Marketers must develop their skill set more thoroughly due to reducing their sector. One of these misconceptions is that growth hackers solely use analytics, a misperception many outsiders hold. While crucial, analytics serves more as a benchmark for competence.

Growth hackers are resourceful and interested in creative growth in addition to data. The most effective growth hackers use their left and right brains to build firms profitably and originally.

Like pumping gas into the little balloon's hole to fill it to its maximum capacity, these people limit their attention and build on the tiniest bit of success.

Chapter 7

Constructing A Funnel

A funnel has a large end that narrows into a triangle form, much like a bottleneck, before having a tiny aperture. To make recalcitrant materials collaborate appropriately, funnels are required while filtering them.

When it comes to client funneling, the objective is often to remove the erratic people to discover those looking for your product or certain information.

You'll want to direct site visitors, so they arrive at a registration or checkout page and are invited into your community.

Imagine the first objective of "Inviting Visitors" as being at the wide end of the funnel; these visitors may be fans or people who have just stumbled onto the site for the first time. In either case, the objective is to establish a connection with potential group members.

In light of this, the next stage would be to

"Activate Members," which entails developing a connection with a client or prospective client. It would be the third stage to "Retain the Customer."

Three-Step Process

Consider the first three stages as the start of a relationship. Activity on the part of the visitors leads to the first step (inviting them). Consider that this lovely person is flirting with you across the table. Like a wink, new users must sign up for an email list, make an account, or make a transaction on the website.

The user will then be required to continue using the product in the next phase (Activate Members), much like in a love relationship where dates are expected. This may include those who regularly read and distribute emails or make purchases of goods. These users (Retain the Customer) are the most similar to newlyweds.

Recognizing Success Rates

A situation where thousands of people visit the website, but just a few make purchases might be depressing.

It's critical to comprehend which dialogue rates in this situation indicate typical achievement. Honestly, there is less traffic as you get farther down the funnel. Mathematically, consider a 100,000-visitor site with a conversion rate of 1%, or 1,000 subscribers.

Let's say that just 600 of the 1,000 people decide to stay, which is a 60% conversion. Although the data may be used to assess personal development, it is almost difficult to compare them across individuals.

Understanding the Variables

If a product is explicitly associated with your total traffic, that should be your first consideration. Many people will soon go on to something else if the product is an ebook about carpentry but the contents are about welding.

The relationships between the offered items and the headlines of feature articles heavily influence this. In light of this, certain traffic sources have the potential to convert members at a faster rate than others.

This may sometimes be current hot issues or numerous other instances.

Think about your unique activation objective in a different setting. Making an email request is significantly simpler than making a sale. Greater outcomes come from requesting fewer favors. High membership costs also fall under this category.

It's crucial to consider other companies operating in the same industry while analyzing retention rates. More recurring customers will utilize certain items than others.

A fruit-of-the-month club will urge people to buy items each month, but high-end hand-crafted furniture pieces may not have repeat customers.

Identifying Success

Once a growth hacker is aware of the factors, there are still more considerations to make while measuring and accelerating growth. The first criterion is that the numbers must always keep rising.

A monthly training regimen should never be

slowed down or shortened like an athlete. Analytics-wise, the number of visitors should increase steadily each month. This has nothing to do with the unknowns since growth should proceed as planned, notwithstanding any experiments in trial and error.

After establishing consistent development, think about monitoring progress with a fellow hacker. Find a company that has a product in a related sector but doesn't directly compete with yours and collaborates to identify the growth rates that will be most successful.

To ensure the success of both of your enterprises, compare your financials. These examples could be more applicable to local enterprises, such as New York and Los Angeles coffee shops. Another example may be two internet retailers of winter clothing, one of which offers scarves and the other hats. Realistic conversion rates may be determined using these techniques.

Finally, confirm that you are accurately reading the data. Instead of focusing on the loss in retention, consider this properly if visitor numbers rise, but retention falls.

The primary objective of collecting this data is to

provide conversion rates at several critical stages along the funnel. Over time, these distinct phases will interact to have a bigger effect on the company.

Placing a priority

Funnels assist in deciding where to focus attention to foster development. The analytics often includes outcomes, even while procedures are still not solid.

With just 100 new visitors daily, consider a 60 percent discussion rate from visitors to members and a 50 percent conversion rate from those members to users. The emphasis of the growth hacker, in this case, should be on the high discussion rates in contrast to the low numbers of new visitors.

Now that growth has been set aside, it's time to reflect on the product. "Product-market fit" refers to a product's position in the marketplace.

In other words, it could be time to reconsider the product if it fully vanishes from the market and 40% of its consumers aren't upset.

The development team should put more effort into the product itself, working to produce something that would provoke uproar if it ever left the shelves (online or otherwise). Ensure that any energy invested in a product's development goes toward a product that merits it.

Chapter 8

Increasing Visitors

Many people will skip this chapter and assume that growth hacking's primary objective is to increase traffic. While more traffic is essential and a major outcome for expanding an online company via traffic, it is simply the final destination; the trip itself is worthwhile and advised.

Regardless of where you are in this chapter, it's time to get down to business and cover the four processes that make up the essentials:

1, 2, 3, P

The first strategy is to pull in traffic. There are three methods to generate traffic to your website, and each one starts with the letter "P." Simply defined, this is a means for you to draw people by giving them a cause to keep coming back to the website.

Users will be pulled to the site and eager for more

information, whether you pique their interest with facts, provide incentives in the form of rewards or presents, or give away a free book.

The Push technique is the following kind. Consider Pull as a door with the word "Welcome" on it, and Push as a person handing out invitations. With Push, growth hackers bypass the allurements and approach consumers directly, forcing them to their website.

Consider those people, for instance, who are eager to watch a new YouTube video but are informed that they must first see a sponsored advertisement.

Advertisement. Push marketing is locating prospective customers and directing them to your website.

Product is denoted by the final "P." Through a social networking platform like Facebook, this strategy may be explained in the simplest possible manner. In essence, the product may spread faster the more individuals utilize it. This holds for any program, such as Words With Friends, Snapchat, or Instagram, that compels users to communicate with other "friends" somehow.

Examining the Techniques

Growth hackers can analyze which trails of online distribution are expanding and in which direction, and both push and pull approaches challenge them to reconsider the concept of "distribution."

Simply investigate which web portals are most popular for folks with less expertise. There are methods for figuring out which places are more welcoming and convenient for group gatherings, like a well-known restaurant.

Knowing where visitors gather can help you choose how and where to attract them to your website. But with the product approach, distribution stays the same, but the definition of "product" may be altered to include additional people.

This holds for the sort of clients and the growth hacker in the issue. Growth hacking may modify the goal or definition to apply to other people, but it cannot change the product itself.

Additionally, no one way works better than the others in terms of effectiveness; each depends on the product and the hacker, with certain items requiring a combination of all three for success.

Top Pull Techniques

Being a featured blogger or guest blogger on another person's site is perhaps one of the most well-known Pull strategies. These techniques are excellent for driving traffic, particularly since blogs' SEO context enables search engines like Google to look for certain terms to emphasize the articles, keywords, and items mentioned. With these techniques, you have more possibilities to get found in the search the more you publish (daily articles, for example). However, the most successful blogs continue to emphasize specializing.

Growth hackers may concentrate on podcasting or guest podcasting in addition to blogging. Podcasts, like blogs, regularly disseminate information to target audiences interested in that kind of content.

Podcasts, as opposed to blogs, can expand listening and reading horizons. Assuming the target audience listens to every episode, guest podcasters may connect with a particular audience through podcasts. However, one disadvantage of guest podcasting is that, unlike clicking on text inside a printed piece, podcasts are not often indexed like those from SEO, and links or companies mentioned are difficult to locate.

Then there are manuals, whitepapers, and ebooks, all of which may be purchased or distributed for no cost. A nicely designed, well-written book on a specialized topic is more difficult to pass through than a blog post, which is simple.

Free books often persuade readers to register for a website to get the book. Giving over their email address in return for a free ebook will seem like a fair transaction to users. Additionally, they are readily spreadable through social media platforms, encouraging online writers to share their work with those who have similar interests.

Infographics are another pull tactic that is often quite popular with new users. These exquisitely crafted visualizations may showcase data in addition to design and entice people to share them on social media.

When creating an infographic, consider selecting a fascinating subject with recent data. Create the story, choose a design aesthetic emphasizing the idea, and polish the design and content before disseminating it. Infographics that include pictures and direct viewers to the original publishing site are popular on websites like Pinterest.

Webinars are a kind of online seminar that welcomes participants from all over the globe to learn more about a topic in an environment that resembles a classroom. Typically held life, webinars are planned as an occasion for participants to anticipate and invite their friends through simulcast. These kinds of pulls often ask individuals serious about participating and are invite-only with restricted seating to make it seem more like an event. These strategies serve as a win-win relationship between companies and customers since they are informative.

Social media use has been mentioned sporadically throughout the book, but it's crucial to remember that it's more than simply flavoring. While there are numerous things to avoid, there are also other things to concentrate on, such as participating in People who often provide value and fit your product's target market.

Always respond to queries from customers and provide suggestions. Relationships will be formed, and your business will learn what products its clients want to see next. Let your imagination go wild on social media, but remember to approach it more like a marathon than a sprint.

Consider employing competitions in addition to social media to increase visitors. Both small and big businesses benefit from contests. When running a contest, the objective is to reward your expanding audience with something valuable and important.

Not every site should give free the most recent technology, particularly if it intends to sell something that doesn't need it. To give customers the impression that they have a greater chance of winning, choose the perfect grand prize and provide something for first, second, and third.

Make a great deal by picking a winner and letting everyone know the award is genuine.

Chapter 9

Recognizing Pushback Tactics

Consider switching to push techniques after you have mastered pull methods. In contrast, push tactics require some kind of disruption to pull techniques, which entail an inducement.

When considering a push technique, picture a YouTube advertisement. Although the advertisement is not what the user wanted, they must view it before playing the movie they intended to watch. Push seeks people by going out and looking for them, while Pull brings them inside.

It's critical to comprehend the lifetime worth of a client before using push tactics. A consumer's total profit during their lifetime is known as LTV. Since LTV, Starbucks can open a shop on every corner since each one represents a certain amount of lifelong consumers.

According to the calculation, certain items will generate a specific revenue each year. Still, they could be part of a product whose consumers only switch every five years, meaning their total LTV is only valid for those five years.

Pushback Methods

Buying ads like the ones discussed that play before YouTube videos is perhaps the most well-known push technique. There is a time and place for everything, and growth is the ultimate aim, even if they appear more like marketing than actual growth hacking.

However, when purchasing advertising, there is still room for imagination and strategy in terms of both when and where to post an ad. In addition to the industry giants like Google, specialized websites that are more closely related to certain items should also be considered when advertising. Remember the platform, ad calendar, and demographic profiles when purchasing advertisements.

The next push method is the promo exchange when two businesses both mention the other's product to swiftly expand awareness of one while assisting the expansion of the other. This works best when you locate another business with a comparable clientele.

While there are numerous effective strategies to carry out a promo exchange, think about starting by exchanging tweets or Facebook posts. There are dedicated and sponsored email swaps in the world of email. A dedicated email devotes its full content to a different company, while an email exchange often simply includes a connecting, "sponsored by" message. Swaps for giveaways and ad space are further variations.

Recruiting affiliates would be another push strategy. Essentially, this technique sets up a chart where you compensate someone for each achievement. Milestones may be whatever you choose, but they often revolve around driving traffic to your website or reactivating existing members.

Affiliates may use various strategies to drive traffic, but the key concept is that you pay them to do it rather than doing the task yourself. If you're off looking for a critical partner, be sure to properly investigate the person.

To discover something that reflects your brand, your product, and your business.

Finally, push growth hacking also includes direct sales. While direct sales teams are not effective for all products, they are effective for some and shouldn't be entirely ignored. Consider appstack.com, even though most entrepreneurs prefer to avoid these strategies. This firm started with local business mobile advertisements but started with telephone sales. This is less frequent in the contemporary digital environment, but it still exists and may be effective for some.

Chapter 10

Implementing Product Tactics

The product technique of expansion is perhaps the most sophisticated. Using the real product is one of the most engaging ways to share a product and expand a company, even if push and pull tactics are equally successful. Compared to any push or pull tactics, the huge impacts that come from product ways are unmatched.

Pull approaches have the terrible side effect of maybe losing the traffic-generating folks. When employing an infographic to increase traffic, remember that daily incoming traffic may decline since most people only interact with an infographic a few times.

But if you use the product, it's completely feasible that each time you visit the website, you won't just be welcoming back a previous client; you'll also be welcoming your whole online network. A product or service is said to have gone viral when every user brings another user with them when they return.

In business terms, the infectious cycle is relevant if a growth hacker can create a network where each product user invites a second user, which equals a coefficient greater than 1, or "K," which is synonymous with exponential growth.

Since even the most skilled strategies do not always succeed for every product or market, coefficients as high as 1 are uncommon in most cases, for instance, in B2B businesses. However,

It's crucial to remember that any K factor over 0 leads to positive development, notwithstanding the odds.

Product Marketing

Social networks surround us, and sending out network invites is a fantastic method to showcase your goods. The most well-known social networks are probably Twitter, Facebook, Gmail, and LinkedIn, but others are gaining popularity quickly. Remember to consider all of your options when considering these network invites, including your phone contacts, email connections, and social contacts.

A button that allows users to instantly invite all

their friends is becoming increasingly common in mobile applications. Similarly, email lists and social media connections operate in the same manner. You will discover that these numbers soon pile up to reach large audiences, even if just a small number of people download the app at first but choose to share it with their hundreds of friends.

In social sharing, which differs slightly from the abovementioned approach, users only let others mention a product or service inside their network.

For instance, this approach merely requests that users mention the product in their profile or status so that others may see it and, perhaps, click on it instead of asking them to tell their friends to "Like" your page.

These are often accessible in the form of buttons below a posting, for instance, on a blog. Along with the number of people who have shared the subject or article, there will be an example, such as Like, Tweet, or Share. In terms of analytics, this information is also relevant. If your traffic is mostly

If it originates from Twitter, it also enables people to publish on other sites.

API Integrations combine goods more thoroughly than social sharing. Instead of requesting authorization before sharing, API Integrations design an environment that allows users to do so automatically and without being constantly reminded. Take the music-based app and website Spotify as an example. Anyone linked to Spotify and Facebook will instantly have their Facebook feed published. Only open authorization makes this kind of frictionless sharing possible. Another example is the Nike+ app, which is also connected to Facebook.

With the help of this software, runners can easily post their routes and finishing times online to encourage one another and foster competitiveness. The dominating side holding the reins is perhaps the only drawback to these strategies. In other words, Facebook will always share with others to promote its message. Still, it may exclude others from its information to maintain its position as the largest and finest.

One of the first forms of growth hacking was the choice of backlinks. A service called "Get your free email at Hotmail" was introduced by the company, encouraging others outside of their group to sign up and start a viral chain. Any widget or side panel may be thought of as a backlink. Another example is guest posts, which are still as powerful as ever.

In growth marketing, the company Dropbox often comes to mind when the term incentive is used. After months of adversity, the team adopted a strategy to distribute vacant space.

Simply by signing up friends, the audience. In this sense, their storage space soon transformed into a kind of payment, motivating visitors to join and share with friends to get more storage space for data.

The corporation gains new customers via Dropbox, which adds value, and the users get free storage space, which is important to them. Many other businesses made unsuccessful attempts to mimic Dropbox. Perhaps one of the reasons is that Dropbox gave extra space free by evaluating knowledgeable customers and provided greater prizes to those who knew their software better.

Then there is natural word-of-mouth. One of the best strategies is still for people to recommend your product to others, whether online or offline, and this only occurs when consumers really like a product. This approach may or may not be the product of a planned growth marketing attack.

Even without rewards, these people are willing to spread the news. Both measurement and control are impossible with this kind of methodology. Consider telling someone about a new technology or movie coming out, but only before you look forward to it.

There are specific actions that may increase the likelihood of word-of-mouth advertising even when these strategies seem random. Think about developing stunning things that have a straightforward attitude. Other organic products come in both stylish and efficient pain-relieving varieties. Finally, original, interesting, and emotionally engaging items may sometimes spread swiftly and without much effort.

Conclusion

Making Members Active

While attracting visitors to a website has been a significant part of the trip, they are more of a problem than a solution. It's time to mobilize members rather than just have tourists circle the area.

Unfortunately, visitors that simply stop by will depart quite often. As a result, activation is the ultimate objective. Visitors are activated when they do an action you have predetermined for them to accomplish.

The goal of these strategies, which may cover various topics, is to pique the visitors' curiosity beyond what they see on the website's surface.

There are other strategies, but the primary goal is often to encourage a visitor to input an email address or make a purchase.

Consider encouraging visitors to read a blog, leave a comment, do a survey, view a video, engage with another user, or seek some type of friendship or membership in addition to the two methods mentioned above.

Even if they seem straightforward, growth marketing sometimes just needs modest outcomes. Keep in mind that many modest outcomes add up to many enormous results. Consistency is vital, as is continuing to strive for ever-higher objectives.

Summary

Programming and Internet marketing are no longer two distinct fields. The practice of growth hacking combines the techniques and steps utilized for each.

Businesses of all sizes are increasingly looking for growth hackers to help them expand to tremendous success on an exponential scale that seems to happen overnight.

Initially, IT specialists and, business students, internet marketers are now using a variety of hacking tactics to operate underground.

Thanks to technological advancements, a keyboard, and the ever-expanding global Internet are now at anyone's fingertips, making growth hacking possible.

People are encouraged to create portfolios throughout their undergraduate careers, whether it is via internships, freelancing, or working for themselves as Internet-savvy fanboys.

The greatest work of a designer must be highlighted in a portfolio, which may be of any kind or degree.

Many freelancing industries allow for the creation of portfolios, but it's crucial to always employ correct language and spelling skills. Additionally, it's a good idea to sometimes go back and edit older work using fresh strategies you've learned along the road.

The open-ended ambition that a well-maintained portfolio inspires may be the most significant component of any portfolio. Future employers are curious about where you want your career to go and support the foundation with that goal in mind.

A particular specialization within the portfolio often benefits both people and enterprises. Even the tiniest businesses may get high search results on the biggest search engines by developing a specific niche, as indicated in the long tail of keywords.

A firm's success is considerably enhanced by narrowing the company's emphasis while maintaining a straightforward marketing approach among current and potential clients.

Numerous examples already exist, and plenty more are on the horizon. Examine areas that now pique your interest while searching for a specialty. To learn more, think about acquiring specialized periodicals or doing in-depth study.

Business-minded people will immediately think of innovative strategies to advance subcategories within their chosen area. Others will only wish to write about the topic to share their expertise with the world and build a community of extra people who share their interests.

There are four ways to launch a company after a product has been developed that are always in demand. Always put relationships first. Customers value established ties, which helps everyone, from brick-and-mortar pizza restaurants to internet teapot sales in Taiwan.

Another crucial element is direct response copywriting, which shouldn't be approached subtly. To draw in visitors, it's crucial to have catchy, tagline-like headlines in our millisecond world.

The third strategy for success, content marketing, requires users to regularly send out material to their audience in a manner that makes them eagerly anticipate emails and other information.

Finally, make sure your items are worthwhile. In this situation, value is significant in terms of worth rather than money. Avoid wasting your time or your customers' time by blogging, creating articles, or promoting a subpar product.

Growth hackers know that "going viral" is not a random phenomenon. Any film or product receiving millions of views is more successful than a one-hit-wonder. Only a quality product with strong confidence can become viral.

Growth hackers might set specific, doable objectives after locating the appropriate product. Analytics will be used to direct these objectives, prioritizing each company's strengths for ultimate success.

Any hypothesis has the potential to be incorrect, but those having a specific goal and supporting data are more likely to be correct. Growth hackers may demonstrate results via these marketing experiments and replicate them as required to obtain the optimum outcomes for outstanding results.

Additionally, it's critical to comprehend customer psychology to measure progress. Growth hackers know how to use a funnel to direct infrequent users to the website to locate individuals prepared to register for an email account or make repeat purchases.

Increasing traffic is essential for growth hacking. Growth hackers may push and lure consumers to a site using different marketing strategies.

Push methods pursue new clients with marketing, while methods utilize rewarded strategies.

The product method is another approach, and it's arguably the most effective. This covers systems where users must be logged in to utilize a certain service, like Facebook and Twitter.

Finally, keep in mind that just having visitors to a website is not enough. Bringing in new visitors and funneling existing ones through the website is crucial. You may start as a successful growth hacker by asking visitors to read a blog, click on a link, view a video, or register for an account.

Other Books By Joseph H. Carillo

1. The Power Of Positive Mindset: Overcoming Negativity To Pursue A More Meaningful Life
2. Magnetic Therapy: Unveiling the Electromagnetic Healing Power
3. Speak With Confidence: An Introduction To Becoming A Public Speaking Star By Captivating Your Audience
4. Knowledge vs Action: Shift Your Mindset, Take Charge Of Your Actions, And Create The Life You Desire

One Last Thing...

Dear Reader,

I hope you enjoyed reading this book and found it to be valuable for your needs. As an author, it means a lot to me when readers take the time to leave a review on Amazon. Your feedback not only helps me improve my writing but also helps potential readers decide if this book is right for them.

If you have a few minutes to spare, I would greatly appreciate it if you could leave a review on Amazon. Your honest opinion can help other readers make informed decisions and can make a real difference in the success of this book.

To leave a review, simply search for the book title and my name on Amazon.com, and select the book from the search results. Once you have navigated to the book's page, scroll down to the review section and share your thoughts on the book.

Rest assured that every single review is personally read and appreciated by me. Your feedback is crucial in helping me understand what worked well and what could be improved upon in future editions. Thank you in advance for your support and for taking the time to leave a review.

Best regards,

Joseph H. Carillo

www.ingramcontent.com/pod-product-compliance
Lightning Source LLC
Chambersburg PA
CBHW070456220526
45466CB00004B/1851